D1830274

HOW MARX FAILED IN HINDU INDIA

HOW MARX FAILED IN HINDU INDIA

V.T. Rajshekar

GYAN

© **Author**
All rights reserved. No part of this book may be reproduced, stored, adapted, or transmitted in any form or by any means, electronic, mechanical, photocopying, micro-filming, recording or otherwise, or translated in any language, without the prior written permission of the copyright owner and the publisher. The book is sold subject to the condition that it shall not, by way of trade or otherwise, be lent, resold, hired out, or otherwise circulated without the prior publisher's written consent in any form of binding or cover other than that in which it is published.

The views and opinions expressed in this book are author(s) own and the facts reported by them have been verified to the extent possible, and the publishers are not in any way liable for the same.

ISBN : 978-81-212-1291-5

First Published, 2015

Gyan Publishing House
23, Main Ansari Road, Darya Ganj,
New Delhi- 110 002
Ph. : 2328 2060, 2326 1060
E-mail: books@gyanbooks.com

: Reliable Infomedia, New Delhi

Cataloging in Publication Data—DK
Courtesy: D.K. Agencies (P) Ltd. <docinfo@dkagencies.com>

Rajshekar Shetty, V. T., 1932- **author.**
How Marx failed in Hindu India / V.T. Rajshekar.
pages cm
Reprint.
ISBN 9788121212915

1. Socialism and Hinduism—India. 2. Hinduism and politics—India. I. Title.

DDC 335.40954 23

CONTENTS

PREFACE TO FIRST EDITION—1978

A gigantic country like India with a mammoth 600-million population—fast going downhill—should be a matter of international concern. For the first time after Independence, the country has reached a zero growth rate.

There have been such an all-round deterioration—economic, social, cultural, political, educational and even moral—that this country with a so-called " glorious cultural heritage " is now being called the " Sick Man of Asia ".

While the plight of the Untouchables and tribals, forming one-third of the country's population, and the " Other Backward Classes " has dipped to rock bottom, the other 10% of the elitist population is enjoying unprecedented prosperity—monopolising the whole gamut of day-to-day activity.

And yet the whole mass of humanity in this subcontinent has shown no sign of unrest—let alone a desire to better its lot. The country looks a picture of contentment and perfect peace. This is the wonder of all wonders at a time when country after country is getting liberated in dramatic sequence.

India has thus become a sociological wonder to the whole world. While the thinking sections the world over are worried about this country, " Hindu India " is totally indifferent, if not somewhat philosophical. What are the reasons for this peace of the graveyard that is India ? It is these that I have sought to analyse in this thesis which will be equally topical in the country's existing political situation caught between Mrs. Gandhi's fake socialism and Jayaprakash Narayan's bogus " Total Revolution "—with the C.P.I. and the C.P.M. more busy running at each others throat rather than crushing its enemies.

The outline was published in a prestigious New Delhi journal some years ago and the tremendous reaction that it created when this stark truth was exposed to public gaze and the encouragement that I got from the country's sociologists, Marxian thinkers, Dalits and fellow journalists made me develop the thesis into a book form. I can dare say that this is the first time that anybody is coming out with this theory to explain the failure of the Indian Left movement. Since its publication is delayed, many friends desired to have this outline.

I will be the happiest person if this booklet provokes a debate and a heart-searching among our Left leadership and particularly the cadres.

BANGALORE
May, 1, 1978

V. T. RAJSHEKAR

PREFACE TO SECOND ENLARGED EDITION—1988

India, as this is written, can be likened to a vast lunatic asylum. As the slaves of India—Scheduled Castes, Scheduled Tribes, Backward Castes, and religious minorities like Muslims, Christians, Sikhs, over 85% of the population—are busy sincerely doing their assigned work, the upper caste rulers (15%) are busy quarrelling among themselves though they are all united in enslaving the rest.

So in this situation, we can blame none except the Marxist leadership. This book tries to explain how Marxism failed in "Hindu India". I reproduce my article in the prestigious Indian daily, *Statesman* (Nov. 4, 1987), "Why Marx Failed in Hindu India", as part of my preface to this book. The very fact that this article was not challenged by the Marxist leadership proves that Marxism in India has become a business :—

India's biggest tragedy is not its failure to banish poverty or even its centuries-old caste system, but the failure of Marxism. As a student I was attracted to Marxism and read every available Marxist text sincerely, believing that India would soon have its long-awaited revolution which would sweep away inequality and poverty. For years I dreamt of revolution and yearned for it. But that elusive revolution never came.

Though I never formally joined the Communist Party I was virtually taken for a member. I used to be invited even to some "cell meetings". My father was a Special Magistrate appointed to try Communist cases in the 1950s in Mangalore but I supported the Marxist "revolutionaries" both in evading arrest and in other legal matters. I held Communist leaders in great reverence. A. K. Gopalan and S. A. Dange were my heroes. In those days we never thought of caste. To us "class" was the greatest barrier and "class struggle" our dream.

Feet of Clay

But, alas, all that soon faded away. My dreams were shattered. When I became a newspaper reporter and got an opportunity to watch these revolutionaries with feet of clay, I soon learnt that all that glitters is not gold. Yet I hoped against hope. Under the influence of Krishna Menon, the then Defence Minister, contesting the famous North Bombay election in 1961, I resigned from the *Indian Express* and joined "India's first Leftist English daily" *Patriot*, in Delhi. I was one among the few "comrades" selected by Krishna Menon who dubbed all other newspapers the "jute Press" and believed that *Patriot* would be a breakthrough in Indian journalism.

Within a year things went sour. I learnt for the first time how the upper castes used Communism for their selfish ends. I am being a little autobiographical just to impress the point how my high hopes were dashed to the ground and also to echo the feelings of millions of my other countrymen, particularly the Dalits.

Mr. Dange, the founder-chairman of the undivided Communist Party of India and winner of the Lenin Prize, was himself expelled from the party for his claim that all the wisdom of Karl Marx was derived from the Vedanta. Mr. E. M. S. Namboodiripad presented an idol of Parasurama (a puranic Brahmin hero who claimed to have killed all the Kshatriyas in the world with his axe and after whom Mr. Namboodiripad's State of Kerala was called "Parusuram Shrusti") to Mao Zhedong in Beijing. In his latest book, "Reminiscences of a Communist", Mr. Namboodiripad often refers to his Brahmin background. The point I am making is that even such eminent Marxist leaders are not able to get over their caste background. Decasteing is more important than de-classing.

In Andhra Pradesh, till Mr. N. T. Rama Rao brought political power to his Khammas, the Communist Party was called Khamma Party because the other dominant caste—the Reddys—were all in the Congress. To fight the Reddys, the Khammas joined the Communist Party. In Kerala, the Marxist leadership promised to make Mrs. K. R. Gowri the Chief Minister and because of this the Left Democratic Front won the recent Assembly election, but they abandoned her after coming to power. This disappointed the Ezhavas who constitute the single largest caste group in Kerala and have always been the backbone of the Marxist movement.

The caste composition of the State Assembly in Kerala demonstrates the upper caste bias of the leadership.

I can go on giving any number of examples to prove how the CPI and CPI(M) leadership and even some of the Naxalite groups have given up the Marxist path which would hurt the interests of the upper castes. Trade unionism is used to promote upper caste interests while low paid rural labour is neglected. Marxist journals are full of irrelevancies and contain nothing that is of interest to the vast majority of the oppressed people.

They are more concerned about the Communist struggle in other countries but remain silent about the Left's great betrayal in India. The parliamentary rather than the revolutionary path has been adopted because such compromises ideally suit the upper caste Left leadership. So much so the Left-leaning Dalits and tribals feel that the Indian Communists are not real Marxists.

The Communist leadership today has stopped talking of revolution. The police are no longer afraid of Communists. Land reform has been forgotten. When the Mandal Commission on the Backward Classes met Mr. Jyoti Basu, he said that there was no need for the Commission to tour West Bengal as there was no caste problem in the State and the backward classes were well treated. But he had no answer when Mr. B. P. Mandal showed him the hundreds of petitions he had received during his tour of West Bengal.

The problem with our Communist leadership is that it has deliberately strayed from the Marxist-Leninist path because it is not prepared to betray Brahminism. Caste became dearer to it than the country. Today, the country's revolutionary sections namely the Scheduled Castes (20%), Scheduled Tribes (10%), Backward Castes (40%), Muslims (15%), Christians (2.5%) and Sikhs (2%), who are yearning for social change, feel betrayed. In every struggle by these sections the Marxist leadership has been on the opposite side. There is nothing wrong with the Communist cadres. The fault lies with the leadership.

Caste System

Nowhere in the world is the situation so ripe for revolution as in India. But the caste system stands in the way of turmoil.

So what India needs is a thorough-going cultural revolution to pull down caste and the corrput value system that supports this structure. The contradictions are there in plenty, but our Marxist leadership does nothing to sharpen them. On the other hand, in some places the Marxist leadership actively obstructs revolution. The problem with this leadership is that it is not even prepared to tolerate honest criticism let alone take corrective action. No wonder few take our Communist parties seriously.

The role played by the Marxist leadership on the Muslim personal law dispute, the Sikh nationality question and the Dalit struggle are classic instances of betrayal. Their stand on Jharkhand, Gorkhaland and the reservations question is no different from that of the BJP. It is this betrayal that has forced the oppressed religious and national minorities to look for alternatives in the philosophy of Babasaheb Ambedkar, Mahatma Phule, E. V. Ramaswamy, Ram Manohar Lohia and Sri Narayana Guru all of whom have aruged that it is not possible to break "class" without breaking "caste", said the *Statesman* article.

The popularity of this book proves that people by and large have accepted our thesis. As this is written Marxism is practically dead in India. The two major communist parties are not taken seriously. The "Marxist" Governments in West Bengal and Kerala are behaving like any other bourgeois governments. We have a fear that in course of time the enslaved people of India will have to first fight these "Marxists". Because Marxism in India is being employed to preserve and perpetuate brahminism.

Even the two giant communist countries, Soviet Russia and China, have compromised with our lifeless Indian "communist" parties. To be in the good books of the upper caste rulers of India, these two communist countries have compromised with the CPI and CPM. So if the Indian slaves are cheated of revolution the blame goes not only to the Indian "Marxist" leadership but also to USSR and China.

And it is this failure that must make the enslaved people to think of an alternative path to Indian Revolution.

September 1, 1988 — V. T. RAJSHEKAR
Bangalore, India.

1. INTRODUCTION

Let not anybody mistake that this is an anti-communist tirade by a bourgeois agent. Yes. Such a charge was hurled at us by some people when an article under a slightly different title appeared in a Delhi journal (*Caravan*) in 1974. The article provoked a big controversy and became the subject of debate in many communist circles. Many people dubbed us anti-Marxist and said that this was an article written at the instance of agent provocateurs. But the same journal published over 15 letters endorsing the thesis and a majority of them were from Marxists themselves. Besides, we also received a letter from the late A. K. Gopalan, who was then ailing at the Vellore Hospital, also endorsing the thesis. We had discussions with P. Sundarayya, Jyoti Basu and all of them agreed with us in principle. And this is what emboldens us to further elaborate the thesis and we hope our observations will be taken in the right sense as a well-wisher of the Left movement. *We want to assure that we are not against Marxism but against the upper caste Marxist leadership that destroyed Marxism in India.*

Our friends in the CPI, CPM and the Naxalite groups know us and our philosophy too well. They all are convinced about our concern and keen interest in Marxism. Therefore, let not anybody mistake us as a communist-baiter. We have great faith in Marxism and we have sincerely worked for revolution in our own humble way. After making our stand clear to ward off any possible misinterpretation of the thesis, we will now proceed to state the case.

Revolution

World history has amply proved that to this day no superior political philosophy has emerged excelling Marxism-Leninism-Maoism. Over half the world population is under the spell of this philosophy and as days pass more and more countries are coming under its influence. Millions of people in the non-communist world are craving for Marxism.

But what is the position in India? No other country in the world is more ripe for revolution than India. Jayaprakash

Narayan had repeatedly said that the country was fast heading towards revolution and then he started his own brand of 'Total Revolution'. Some others said the defeat of Mrs. Indira Gandhi and her Congress Party would trigger off a revolution. The Naxalites groups had circulated leaflets as early as 1974 saying that revolution has begun in India.

Who does not want a "revolution" in India? From the extreme right wing political party to the extreme left Naxalites—everybody wants, everybody hopes for revolution.

Here is a sample of their resolutions:

Lucknow: Printed red leaflets appeared here appealing to the people that without a bloody revolution, progress was not possible. The leaflet was purported to have been published on behalf of the "Anti-Anarchic Element Association", Sitapur. (*Statesman*, New Delhi, Feb. 10, 1974.)

Sarvodaya leader Jayaprakash Narayan said today that the country was fast heading towards a revolution. (*Deccan Herald*, Feb. 3, 1973.)

The CPM Central Committee in a resolution ruled out a smooth, peaceful transition from capitalism to socialism by the use of bourgeoise parliamentary setup. ". . . . such advance could be consolidated and lead to a successful revolution only if the state structure built by the exploiting classes is smashed and a new state power of the toiling people created and the forces of violence and terror unleashed by the counter-revolutionaries met only by a people's army." (*Indian Express*, Nov. 27, 1973.)

K. Kamaraj, Old Congress leader, declared in Madras on Aug. 20, that nothing short of a revolution can cure the economic ills, political dishonesty and degrading morals of the country. (*Indian Express*, Aug. 21, 1973.)

George Fernandes, Chairman of the Socialist Party of India, said at Calicut on Aug. 25, 1973 that the country was on the verge of a revolution due to what he called 27 years of misrule by the Congress.

Like this, we have been reading in the press speeches and resolutions made by all and sundry predicting revolution in India.

We can understand their anxiety for a change. No doubt, people want a change but consciously or unconsciously they are caught in the coil. At no time in the history of the country conditions for a revolution are so ripe as it is today.

Not a day passes without somebody or other saying : "…. at this rate there will soon be a revolution in this country." We are tired of hearing and reading such speeches and statements. But where is that elusive *Revolution* ?

Vijayawada Resolution

No other country in the world is so ripe for revolution as India. The Central Committee (CC) of the Communist Party (Marxist-Leninist) in a resolution said at Vijayawada that "objectively our country is ripe for revolution as could be seen from the fact that the country is plunging deeper and deeper into economic crisis which exposes the utter rottenness of the system itself". (*Indian Express,* April 5, 1974.) The resolution is 14 years old and even today the same ML groups go on talking about this very same elusive revolution. Are they searching for a non-existing black cat in a dark room closing their eyes ?

The poverty and exploitation is so much that for centuries the people are reduced to slavery by a handful of upper caste rulers.

The per capita income of Indians is steadily going down. Since statistics are too familiar and the value of a rupee itself is less than 20 paise, there is no point in giving figures.

Richman's dog

The standard of living of a richman's dog is much higher than that of over 50% of the people of this country. In such circumstances, it is but natural for any optimist to expect a revolution in this country.

Balraj Mehta, writing in the *Indian Express* as far back as June 28, 1974, says : "Can a people be weak, under-nourished, sickly, their vitality sapped and the barest essentials of civilized living denied to them and yet the nation becomes strong ?" Questioning "the false idea" pervading the Indian planning, he says almost every targets set for the Fourth Plan was missed and the Fifth Plan failed to take off even at the launching stage. Since this is written India's economy has nose-dived with more people joining the ranks of paupers.

The adoption of a capital-intensive, luxury-oriented Western technology to a bullock cart economy has created in India a dual society—metropolitan centres of Western-oriented affluence amidst vast expanses of rural poverty. (" Three cheers to Upper caste grave-diggers," *Dalit Voice* editorial, May 16, 1988.) On the one side, we find a small 10% of the comparatively rich, acquisitive, conspicuously consuming, politically powerful, city-centred, "èlite" drawing its ideas and values from the West and on the other side a large mass of " poor" people left out of the circle of production and consumption owing to lack of employment. It is urban boom vs. rural decay. Investments in vital human needs, especially the three basic needs—food, clothing and shelter—have been neglected in the name of lack of finance but investments on the manufacture of luxury items like synthetic fibres, refrigerators, TV sets, computers, liquor, five-star hotels, cinema theatres, entertainment industry is continued recklessly. Our capacity for self-deception must be seen to be believed. We have the strange spectacle of every politician and planner in love with the " poor " but policies made to pamper the rich.

Padmashri for Blackmarketeer

The gulf between the different " classes "—the rich and the poor, the rural and the urban, the educated and the illiterate, the industrial worker and the landless agricultural farmer, the capitalist and the labour, the landlord and the tenant, the white-collared and the manual worker—is increasing day by day. New and newer slums are springing up in every city. According to one survey 25% of a city population lives in slums. Calcutta is a vast slum. Madras, Bombay are following. There is more illiteracy in the country today than in 1947 (year of independence). According to one estimate, India has the largest number of illiterates in the world. If 30% of Indian population is said to be literate, Untouchables and tribals forming 30% of India's population are alomst 100% illiterate.

The little " progress " that we find in India is confined only to the urban area, that too enjoyed by 10% of the élite.

Since our very rulers—the political, social, economic, religious, intellectual leadership—are corrupt from top to bottom, corruption is taken as part of life. Blackmarket, hoarding, adulteration, smuggling, tax-evasion, and black-money, spying for foreign countries are all considered part of our life. Nay, those indulging in these malpractices are paraded as the most respectable citizens of our country. They only get all awards and rewards. Some of them even got Padmashri.

The poverty and misery of India is so much, exploitation by the country's 10% of the élite is so merciless that it is but natural that anybody should predict that a bloody revolution is imminent in India. The country is stagnant. Our rank in the 159-member U.N.O. is 125th while China, which got liberated two years after we became " independent ", today is a mighty super Power—leader of the Third World. There is no point in quoting statistics to give the magnitude of India's poverty because the Government, the Planning Commission and Reserve Bank and everybody knows it, but are deliberately lying to deceive the people. The country is fast sliding back. In the international conclaves India is being described as a beggar nation—because there is no country from which we have not borrowed. India is called the " Sick Man of Asia ". Why not the " Sick Man of the World " ? This is a sick nation, we are a sick society.

Under such circumstances, it is but natural for our padagogues and particularly those in the Left parties to predict that this country will very soon explode in a bloody revolution. To journalists like us, it has become a daily feature to hear such speeches fondly wishing such a revolution.

2. INDIAN REVOLUTIONARIES

Sepoy Mutiny was once considered the beginning of the "Indian Revolution". Communist leaders thought that the historic "Telengana people's armed struggle", the heroic peasant uprising of 1946-51 in which over 4,000 communists and peasant militants were killed, over 10,000 communist cadres jailed and over 50,000 dumped in police camps—was indeed the beginning of the "Indian revolution".

Some communist leaders then thought that this is indeed the beginning of an armed struggle based on the Marxian dialectical and materialistic interpretation of history and class struggle. M. K. Gandhi and Jawaharlal Nehru also thought that the "Indian freedom struggle" would end up in another type of revolution. Similarly, different people including the Naxalites mistook different situations to the beginning of their long-cherished revolution.

But why still there is no revolution? There has never been a shortage of revolutionary figures in this country. Beginning from the Buddha, Basava, Guru Nanak, M. N. Roy, Palme Dutt, Bhagat Singh, Mahatma Phule, Narayana Guru, Subhash Chandra Bose, Dr. B. R. Ambedkar, Lohia, Charu Mazumdar, Periyar Ramaswamy—we had a galaxy of revolutionary figures. Besides, we also have in India a fairly strong Left movement. Beginning from the CPM at the extreme left, we have the pro-Moscow CPI and an assorted lot of socialist parties. The sacrifices made by the leaders of these Left parties to the cause of peasant struggle and working class movement are something very great. Nobody can deny this fact.

Why masses reject Left?

But what did the Left movement in the country achieve? Why have they failed to bring about a revolution in the country? Why did the masses reject the hard-won CPM Governments even in in the Left-leaning Bengal and Kerala—the two bastions of red-revolution? Is it because the Left movement in the country is so badly divided? Has it failed to attract the toiling masses and convince them about the philosophy of "class struggle" and infuse in them a revolutionary zeal? How long the working class can go on pinning hopes on the CPM and the CPI and other Left parties? These are the questions which we have tried to answer in this thesis.

The Left parties in the country particularly the CPM owe an explanation to the people. Let them stop this exercise in futility for a change and do some frank heart-searching as to where exactly they have failed.

A writer in the *Frontier* (Feb. 12, 1977) frankly admitted: "It must be stated that the Indian communist movement is passing through its darkest days. Confusion, hopelessness, division, disintegration and self-suspicion, bordering on self-negation are the chief manifestations. The situation is pretty bad." He adds: "Why is it that the Indian communist movement with 52 long years of history, effort and sacrifice failed to influence the masses significantly, failed to become a decisive force in social life? What are the causes? What is the principal cause among them?"

These are not our words, but that of the *Frontier* —which has years of dedicated service to the cause of Left movement.

3. THE CLASS STRUGGLE THEORY

Let us now examine step by step. The Marxian theory of revolution is based on " class struggle "—a struggle between the different economic " classes ". Emile Burns in *What is Marxism?* explains that Marxism is a general theory of the world in which we live, and of human society as a part of that world. It takes its name from Karl Marx. The Marxist approach to history sees the struggle between contending classes as the principal driving force in the developing of human society. Marx closely examined the struggle of his day and discovered the " laws " of the struggle between " classes ". Class struggle and with it the setting up of state apparatus to protect the interests of the ruling class, came out of a division of human society into " classes " whose interests clashed in production. Class struggle and the state continue through history as long as human society remains divided into " classes ". The very first person to successfully experiment with Marxism and demonstrate to the world its efficacy was V. I. Lenin in Soviet Russia.

Well, it is based on this Marxian theory of " class struggle " that Russia, China and several other countries had their own revolution. Yes, India too has similar " classes " of exploiters and exploited. The poverty and misery of the people here is so much that if India does not have a "revolution" no other country in the world can have it.

This is the firm hope of many Left well-wishers outside the country and the fond desire of those inside too. Thus, India is said to be ripe for " revolution ". People want revolution in this country. Ask anybody he will confidently say that the only solution to this country is a revolution. They long for a revolution. They yearn for a revolution. Even Hindu Nazi counter revolutionaries speak of revolution. Every time there is some burning or looting or for that matter some stray killing in some isolated areas, people say with joy : " Yes, this is the beginning of revolution ". They are so fondly wishing a revolution and confidently predicting one. The " JP movement " in Bihar was hailed as the beginning of the " Indian revolution ". Finally JP died a counter-revolutionary. A number of intellectuals saw in the JP movement a ray of hope for revolution and fondly described the Sarvodaya leader as a combination of Gandhi, Mao and Periyar. At the time of writing, a new " revolutionary " is being flaunted in V. P. Singh. And you can take it from us, he will do everything to prevent the revolution.

Counter-revolutionaries

Marxism has stood the test of time. The very fact that over one-third of the humanity lives under communism testifies to its validity. Even outside these communist countries, the Marxist movement is fairly strong in very many other parts of the world. Until a superior political philosophy disproves the theory of " class struggle " and provides an alternative, Marxism will hold its sway over the world. History has proved the truth of this statement.

Therefore, there is nothing inherently wrong in the Marxian philosophy except for the fact that the " class struggle " theory, which has succeeded in ever so many countries, cannot be applied to " Hindu India ". And that is the reason why the Left movement is limping despite decades of selfless struggle and sacrifice. Not that there is anything basically wrong with the Marxian theory as such, but when Karl Marx propounded his famous theory sitting inside the British Museum in London, perhaps he did not have a personal knowledge of " Hindu India " and its cast-iron caste structure.

Although from the point of view of poverty, exploitation and widening gap between the haves and have-nots, one may jump to the conclusion that a revolutionary situation does exist in India, the actual situation in " Hindu India " is that it is actually in the grip of a grim counter-revolution. What is happening in India today is not a revolution but a multi-pronged revolution against revolution. But our Left leadership has failed to discern it.

What are the different counter-revolutionary movements in India ?

4. CASTE SYSTEM

Marx perhaps did not know that besides the " classes ", India also has the more deadly and diabiolical " castes "—a cunningly devised system that has survived for centuries. Caste system is the bane of " Hindu India ". Even the Buddha, the greatest of all Indians who rebelled against this satanic system, failed to make a dent on this monolith.

Jainism and Buddhism, the very first protest movements against the caste-based brahminism, were soon devoured by this ever hungry gluttonous brahminism and historians soon started interpreting them as " a mere reform movement within Hinduism ". Both Jainism and Buddhism have been since considered as yet another additions to the ever-burgeoning Hindu caste cacophony. Even the Constitution of India says so. That is the beauty of this deathless demon.

Sages and seers come and go on the stage of the great Indian drama but nobody dare touch this killer weed.

" Great reformers and philosophers like Shankaracharya, Raja Ram Mohan Roy, Dayananda Saraswati, and Gandhiji never carried an assault against the fundamentals. In fact they lived all through in caste and died as high-caste men. If one or two of them realised the futility and inequity of caste and declared for a casteless society at the close of their lives, they were murdered by caste fanatics ". (Prof. A. M. Dharmalingam : *Blasted Hopes*, 1951 pp. 92.)

Indian comrades may say that Karl Marx did talk of religion (Marx-Engels : *On Religion*, Progress Publishers, Moscow, 1976), and had made his famous observation : " Religion is the opium of masses ". Lenin wrote long before the Russian revolution : " Religion is one of the forms of spiritual oppression . . . . The weakness of the exploited classes in their struggle against their oppressors inevitably produces a belief in better life after death . . . . Religion teaches those who toil in poverty all their lives to be resigned and patient in this world and consoles them with the hope of reward in heaven .... Religion is the opiate of the people, a sort of spiritual liquor, meant to make the slaves of capitalism drown their humanity and the desires for a decent existence ". (David Shub—*Lenin : A Biography*, Penguin, 1971—pp. 419.)

Both Marx and Lenin were fully aware ot the blinding and poisonous effect of religion on the mental faculty of man. There was religion in Russia and China too. And yet how did these countries have their revolutions ? Yes. This is true. But let us not forget that in these countries there were only " classes " but no " castes ".

In Islamic countries, the Muslims may be divided into many sects. Among Christians too there are scores of faiths. But nobody claims that one sect or faith is superior to the other. The society in Islamic, Christian countries is horizontally divided— " rich " and " poor ".

In a mosque, they may all sit together and pray together. Neither Christians or Muslims have anything like a first-class citizen or a second-class citizen. It is only in " Hindu India " that the society is vertically divided—the whole mass of humanity sandwiched between different water-tight compartments of four major *varnas* and then castes (*jati*) and hundreds of sub-castes each throttling the other to suffocation and centuries of subjugation. The Kaka Kalelkar Commission appointed by the Government of India listed 4,000 castes and sub-castes. No other country in the world has such an ingeniously devised foolproof system. Caste is the foundation on which Hindu religion is built. Karl Marx did not come to India and hence had no first-hand knowledge of India.

The caste system did not stop at merely dividing the society into four major *varnas*. At the bottom of this pyramidical structure, called the " Hindu " society, lies the country's most wretched mass of sub-humans called the Untouchables (fondly called by Gandhi as *Harijans*)—condemned to a gory apartheid for which there is no parallel in the world. It is considered a sin to touch these " heinous " creatures who suffer from the stigma of pollution.

Dr. Ketkar has very graphically depicted the mischief of the Hindu caste system : " ... as long as caste in India does exist,

Hindus will hardly inter-marry or have any social intercourse with outsiders, and if the Hindus migrate to other regions of the earth, the Indian caste would become a world problem ". (Dr. Ketkar on Caste—page 4—quoted from the *Castes in India, their Mechanism, Genesis and Development*, 1916, by Dr. Ambedkar.)

As Dr. M. N. Srinivas, a noted sociologist, puts it : " if and when caste disappears from India, Hinduism will also disappear. " (A Note on Sanskritization and Westernisation—*Far Eastern Quarterly*—1956, Vol. 15—pp. 495). Because, the caste system is the other name for Hinduism.

Sociologists have given the other two important features of the caste system as endogamy and hierarchy.

Economic disparity exists in all the non-socialist countries of the world but the division of society on the basis of status or rank is something peculiar only to " Hindu India ". The Hindu who observes caste, says Taya Zinkin, (*Caste Today*) does so because his religion wants him to ..... The worst legacy of this is the child acquiring the status and caste of his parents. That means a Brahmin is one who is a born Brahmin. A poor man can become rich and vice versa, but in a caste society under Hinduism, there is neither promotion or demotion.

Gandhi upholds Caste

Even the country's Constitution has no objection to the existence of caste. Nay. It offers every facility to perpetuate it. (" The State used to promote Hindu Religion, " DV editorial, Sept. 1, 1987.) Under Article 17, only untouchability is " abolished " (only in letter but not in spirit), but caste is retained. Abolition of caste is not considered the function of the State.

No doubt, Gandhi had condemned the caste. He says : " The caste in so far as it connotes distinctions in status, is an evil." (" Caste "—Mahatma Gandhi—*Young India*—March 23, 1933).

But Bharatan Kumarappa while editing Gandhi's book, *My Religion*, comments : " When he (Gandhi) condemns caste, he condemns only the idea of superiority and inferiority which it came later to acquire. And not the principle of following hereditary occupations which he calls *varna*, and of which he thoroughly approves." A religion that divides man against man and preaches hatred thus found an enthusiastic supporter even in Gandhi, called "Father of the Nation".

The apartheid practiced by the upper castes against the Untouchables is something unparalleled in the world. (V. T. Rajshekar: *Apartheid in India*, 1983, Dalit Sahitya Akademy). Before this, even the "Black problem" of the US pales into insignificance. The American Blacks are, after all, touchables and that is why they are employed as servants in White households. But in "Hindu India" we cannot think of this. An Untouchable cannot come anywhere near the vicinity of an upper caste household since his very presence in the area would lead to pollution. According to the late Baburao Patel, editor of *Mother India*, and an ardent "Hindu": "Every day Hinduism is losing hundreds of Harijans to Islam and Christianity. So far in the last 1,200 years Hinduism has given away over 16 crores of Hindus to these alien religions—of them 99% are converted from *Harijans*. They left Hinduism because the caste Hindus did not want them and tortured them so much that they could no longer survive as Hindus." Largescale conversion of Untouchables (Scheduled Castes as they are called in the Constitution) is going on even to this day and much more vigorously despite the Hindu Nazi efforts to transform the whole world into a land of Hindus.

Historian Tara Chand dealing with the havoc played by the caste system in his book, *A Short History of the Indian People*, (1944) says: The secret of the success of the invaders (Muslim conquerors of the 11th century AD) was the superiority of their social organisation. The Hindu social system had no coherence or unity. Hindus of India were only one in name. The Hindu caste system was based on privilege, on the distinction of high and low, on inequality.... the peoples of India were utterly lacking in unity —religious, political and/or social—their society was based on inequality and hence they were weak". That is why "Hindu India" was successfully under different foreign rulers including the last one, the British, who played one caste against the other and ruled the country for over 300 years.

One White-skinned collector could rule a whole district single-handed and this was because he knew the weaknesses of the people of caste ridden Hindu India and how badly they were divided under the impact of caste hierarchy.

Here is a sample of opinions on the caste system :

M. K. Gandhi : The caste system, as we know, is an anachronism. It must go if both Hinduism and India are to live and grow from day to day (*Young India*).

Tagore : The thing we in India have got to think of is this—to remove those social customs and ideals which have generated a want of self-respect and a complete dependence on those above us—a state of affairs which has been brought about entirely by the domination in India of the caste system, and the blind and lazy habit of relying upon the authority of traditions that are incongruous anachronisms in the present age.

Jawaharlal Nehru : In the context of the society today, the caste system and much that goes with it are wholly incompatible, reactionary, restrictive and barriers to progress. There can be no equality in status and opportunity within its framework, nor can there be political democracy and much less economic democracy. Between these two conceptions conflict is inherent and only one of them can survive. (*Discovery of India*, Chapter VI, page 234.)

P. B. Gajendragadkar : Social inequality and caste loyalty are totally inconsistent with secularism.

Arnold Toynbee : It is evident that this great impact of religiosity on the institution of caste must have seriously aggravated the banefulness of the institution. Caste is always on the verge of being a social enormity, but, when it is keyed up by receiving a religious interpretation and a religious sanction, its enormity is bound to grow to monstrous proportions ..... In the actual event the impact of religion on caste in India has begotten the unparalleled social abuse of untouchability and there has never been any effective movement to abolish or to mitigate untouchability on the part of the Brahmins, the hierarchic caste which become master of the ceremonies of the whole system. (*A Study of History*, 1946—Somerwells abridgement—Vol. I—pp. 350.)

Louis Dumont : It would be an illusion to suppose that the caste could be abolished without bringing any affliction on the

Brahmans. It is inevitable that they should suffer, perhaps unjustly, in the transformation Gandhi professed to desire, simply because they are at the summit of the hierarchy to be abolished. (*Report of the Backward Classes Commission*—1956, page XXV.)

Kaka Kalelkar : The religious caste complex has become so deep-rooted that it is not easy for any caste group to get away from its strong grip. Even the most intellectual including those who declared themselves to be enemies of castes, are not often entirely free, and consciously or unconsciously they act in a manner which gives a fresh lease of life to the caste system. Both by the force of inherited habit and the training imparted to an individual, he feels a deep loyalty to the caste-group. That loyalty is so deep that he is generally unable to shake it off even when he is intellectually convinced that it is baneful. The social differences of caste have become so firm in the mind of the Hindu that he regards them as natural. The two important elements in the Hindu caste system are endogamy and hierarchy. The desire to keep themselves pure is responsible for the rigid observance of endogamy. The feeling of inferiority has resulted in caste hierarchy. (*Report of the Backward Classes Commission*—1956—page 22, vol. 1.)

The Constitution has banned untouchability the practice of which is punishable under law. Gandhi named these " human animals " as *Harijans* and that is the end of the whole thing. Because for the Hindu, the constitution that governs his world is thelaws of Manu which sanction caste and un touchability. Untouchability problem is getting more and more serious and complex day by day. The plight of Untouchables is deteriorating day by day—notwithstanding the reservations in the Constitution.

In India there is a great admiration for everything that is Western. But the Western concepts of liberty, equality and fraternity are not only foreign to the upper castes but they are definitely hostile to them.

Is there anything parallel in the world to this " Hindu " society —the wonder of all wonders ? Can anybody point out in the world a class similar to the sanctified racism of our Untouchables who are sold like cattle, kicked like beasts and yet forming over 20% of the country's population ? And what a fall ! The historians yet called the Hindu society one of the greatest civilisations in the world ! Dr. Babasaheb Ambedkar in a famous speech in 1936 said : " A religion that does not recognise you (Untouchables) as a human being..... is not worthy to be called a religion ".

It is in this special circumstances that a student of Marxism has to view this country. Has any attempt been made to eradicate the canker of caste system ? Some " nationalist " and " patriotic " people in the country may ask : " Why speak of caste ? After all we are living in a casteless society ". Only an unthinking person can make this statement. Upper castes who have achieved everything in life through caste, speak like this. Because it helps them to remain casteless and sometimes even without caste prefix. For those who are yet to climb up the caste ladder, caste is necessary to recognise their " backwardness " which is the cause of their poverty.

Far from taking steps to destroy this cancerous caste system that has played havoc on " Hindu India ", every attempt is being made to nurture this poisonous weed. Political parties including the CPM and the CPI, which say that they are above caste, give election ticket only on the basis of the candidate's caste. Ministers and judges and every other appointments are made in such a way that all upper castes are properly represented. A leader is a leader in " Hindu India " because of his caste and community backing. Every election is fought only on the caste basis. There is no secret about it. The moment we meet a stranger the very first information that we elicit in " Hindu India " is about his caste. Information about a person's caste is the most vital piece of " general knowledge " in today's life. If caste helps us, we go all out to defend it and the moment it harms us we instantly dub a person advocating caste as casteist and communal. Charan Singh was ridiculed as casteist by the upper caste press because he fought for the rights of the Backward Castes.

Talisman

Either this way or that way, caste is very assiduously protected and nurtured since it is the person's caste that can determine his future. Caste is thus a talisman. When the Constitution has itself recognised the caste, what else anybody can do ? So, in the name of caste an eternal warfare is going on from centuries. Each caste is trying to crush the other caste. Numerically smaller but socially " upper castes " are worried that with the increasing awareness among Scheduled Castes, tribals and Backward Castes, coupled with the one-man-one-vote principle of democracy—their centuries-old privileges and positions in the society may crumble. Being at the apex of the caste pyramid, it is these castes that have appropriated all the benefits to themselves while keeping the rest of the society in a permanent pitch darkness. It is this "upper caste" selfishness that caused two caste wars in Gujarat.

The very purpose of the caste system is to maintain social and economic inequality and shower the best of life on the top ten per cent of the population. Barring Brahmins, Kshatriyas and Vaishyas (as *dwijas* these three are marked by cross-thread on their chest) the rest of the no-thread shudras are for centuries condemned to manual work while retaining the brain work to the twice-born *dwijas*. That is the reason why the "Hindus" hate manual work and there is so much rush for the white-collared desk job. Forbidden fruit is always sweet.

Andre Beteille, a noted Indian sociologist, in his book, *Caste, Old and New,* says: "After the advent of democracy, in every range of Indian society a very high value is attached to non-manual work and a white-collared job is viewed as a passport to respectability. This view is all the more keenly held by backward classes who have until recently been almost wholly excluded from such occupations. Now that the white-collared jobs are almost within reach, no price appears to be too high for them."

That means if this Hinduism is allowed to continue, a time may come when no "educated" person will be willing to do manual work. That is why a deliberate and systematic effort is being made to see that literacy is denied to the Backward Castes and the Untouchables. Because the moment a person becomes "educated," he quits his village and runs cityward for a clerical job. The most important part of the upper caste conspiracy is to keep the country permanently illiterate and hence ignorant so that the status quo is preserved. Otherwise, how on earth that over 70% of the country's population is still illiterate despite a specific provision in the very "Directive Principles" of the Constitution to impart "free and compulsory primary education to every child?"

" Caste " cuts across " class "

The unique feature of " Hindu India " is that " classes " cut across " castes ". And " castes " cut across " classes ". There are " poor " people even among Brahmins who stand at the apex of the caste pyramid. But the pity is that these " poor " Brahmins are not prepared to fight the " rich " people of their own caste. This is the case of the " poor " people in every caste and sub-caste and the greatest wonder of the Hindu society is that there are quite a lot of " poor " in every caste and sub-caste.

Apart from this " class ", every caste has a grade and, therefore, even a " low caste " man derives lot of consolation in the fact that in the scale of castes he is " above " some other castes. Because of this gradation, the scaling of castes, it is impossible to organise a common front against the caste system. Every caste derives some benefits from the caste system. How then to excite the " Hindu India " with the Marxian slogan of class struggle ? Karl Marx told the workers of the world to unite : " You have nothing to lose except your chains ", he said. But the artful way in which the social and religious rights are distributed among the different castes, whereby some have more and some have less, makes the Marxian slogan quite useless to whip up the " Hindus " against the caste system. Therefore, in " Hindu India " we cannot have a general mobilisation of the people to attack the caste.

Caste system, therefore, ranks number one among the different counter-revolutionary forces working against revolution.

Merit Theory

Not only literacy is denied to a vast majority, but a new word has been coined to frustrate the efforts of even educated " lower " castes. The word " merit " is nowhere to be found in the Constitution. But the upper castes invented the " merit theory " (V.T. Rajshekar : *Merit, My Foot*, DSA, 1988) to keep out the SC/ST/BCs and religious minorities. The " merit theory " has come as a curse to over 90% of the population which has failed to see through this game.

The upper castes are thus seen bitterly fighting with their back against the wall to retain their magical hold on the masses. In the name of religion, god, *dharma*, and holy scriptures and now

" merit ", they are successfully continuing their traditional work of mental crucifixion of the entire society. In India, one can pass even the most difficult examination and can even be elevated to the highest office of the President of India. But one can never get a promotion from a " lower " caste to an upper caste or even a demotion from an upper caste to a more lowly one.

In parts of erstwhile princely Mysore we were surprised to see fishermen community people doing the traditional temple priests job from generations. But they do not become Brahmins. Coorgs are a great martial race and two among them—Gen. Cariappa and Gen. Thimmaiah—have even become army chiefs. But just because they have been great warriors, they do not become Kshatriyas.

Shivaji's coronation

That there is no promotion from one caste or even sub-caste can be very well illustrated from the classic story of Shivaji —the great 17th century Maratha emperor. When he wanted to perform his coronation ceremony according to Vedic rites, he found to his shock that it was not possible unless he first proved that he was a Kshatriya. Even if he was found to be a Kshatriya, he was past the age of *upanayana* (the sacred thread ceremony) and without the *upanayana* he could not become a Kshatriya. But was he a Kshatriya ? His claim for Kshatriyahood was opposed by the Brahmins, who were led by his Prime Minister Moro Pant Pingle. Shivaji's claim was also in direct conflict with the well-established thesis long insisted upon by the Brahmins that there were no Kshatriyas in the *Kaliyuga.* Shivaji's case is important for several reasons because it proves that the power of determining the status of a " Hindu " depends entirely upon the will of the Brahmin. C. V. Vaidya in his books, *History of Medieval India* and also *Shivaji, the founder of Maratha Swaraj,* gives a vivid description of the way Emperor Shivaji had to bribe the Brahmins to achieve his coronation. This is one such solitary case in " Hindu India " of a shudra being promoted to the rank of a Kashatriya.

Brahmins in Bata Co.

This writer had received scores of letters protesting against calling the Bunts of South Kanara as shudras. (*Illustrated Weekly,* May 6, 1973). They might have resented this " humiliation " but this writer cannot be blamed for this because he was not the creator of the caste system although he could very well appreciate the desire of these protestors to be promoted to the ranks of the Kshatriyas. The desire to get promoted in the caste hierarchy is inherent in every "lower" caste. In the Bata Shoe Co., some of the highest paid officers are Brahmins but that does not mean they can be called Chamars. The Kaka Kalelkar Commission observes: " A Brahmin by doing a tailor's job does not become a tailor by caste nor does he lose his social status if he deals in shoes." This is the beauty of the Hindu caste system.

There is no conversion from a lower caste to a higher one. This is the " Law of Manu " which Dr. Ambedkar once publicly burnt in a bonfire. (*Manawa Dharma Shashtra*—G. C. Haughton, 1982 reprint, Asian Educational Services, C/2/15 SDA, New Delhi-16.)

The Laws of Manu lay down that " obedience to caste rules is the very essence of Dharma". The Shankaracharya of Puri goes on defending caste, untouchability, sati etc. on the basis of the Laws of Manu.

Every religion has a founder but Hinduism has none. There is no religion in the world which is so rich in mythology, symbology, rituals and ceremonies. No foreign power can demolish the caste structure which has stood for centuries like the mighty Himalayas. Hinduism " covers and includes all shades of religious thoughts from monotheism to polytheism and pantheism, from animism to vedantism, from theism to agnosticism and atheism. A Hindu could be a *Dwaitist* or *Adwaitist*, he may worship the primitive Aryan deities or the brahminic deities of the epics and the puranas, or nothing except the self in him. Hindus may be vegetarian, semi-vegetarians (egg and fish-eating kind) or non-vegetarians (meat or beef-eating type). Hindus may be *saivites* or *vaishnavites* the latter belonging either to the northern Sanskrit (*Vadagalai*) or the southern Tamil group (*Tengalai*)." (Prof. A. M. Dharmalingam : *Blasted Hopes*.)

According to Manu, women constituting 51% of " Hindu India's " population " are only cows, mere chattels ". " They can be sold and purchased, they can be even burnt alive along with their husbands' corpses." (*Caravan*, New Delhi, July 11, 1973.)

How much morally degraded were the writers of the so-called " holy scriptures " of the Hindus can be seen from the following few examples taken at random from the *Manu Smriti :*

" The service of the Brahmin is the best duty of the Shudras Therefore, whatever else (the Shudra) he does is useless."

" Whatever is there in this world belongs to the Brahmin, because he is superior by birth ".

Prof. Max Mueller, the greatest German authority on Sanskrit, commenting on the *Brahmanas,* says : " No one would have supposed that at so early a period, and in so primitive a state of society, there could have risen up a literature which for pedantry and downright absurdity can hardly be matched anywhere .... The general character of these works is marked by shallow and insipid grand eloquence, by priestly conceit, and antiquarian pedantry. It is most important that he should know how soon the fresh and healthy growth of a nation can be blighted by priest-craft and superstition. It is most important that he should know that nations are liable to these epidemics in their youth as well as in their dotage. These works deserve to be studied as a physician studies the twaddle of idiots, and the raving of madmen ". (*Ancient Sanskrit Literature*—Panini edition, page 200).

Dr. Babasaheb Ambedkar commenting on the long list of disabilities, accompanied by a most dire system of pains and penalties to which the shudra is subjected to by the brahminic law-givers, says : " .... These disabilities have no parallel anywhere in the world. It is impossible to compare the brahminic law with every other legal system on the point of rights and disabilities." (*Who Were the Shudras,* page 48.) He compares the brahminic law with the Roman Law and says the latter has nothing of the cruelty that characterises the disabilities imposed by the brahminic law.

Gems from the Vedas

Here are some of the selected gems from the Vedic scriptures :

Vasishtha Dharma Sutra : The Veda must not be recited in the presence of a Shudra.

Manu Smriti : A Shudra is not worthy of respect on ground of his wealth of his knowledge no matter how high they are. (Chapter II. versus 135-137.)

Brihaspati Smriti : A Shudra teaching the precepts of religion or uttering the words of Veda, or insulting a Brahmin shall be punished by cutting out his tongue. (Chapter XII. verse 12.)

Gautama Dharma Sutra : Now if he listens to (a recitation of) the Veda, his ears shall be filled with (molten) tin or lac. If he recites (Vedic texts), his tongue shall be cut out. If he remembers them, his body shall be split in twain. (Chapter XX, Sutras 4-6.)

Manu Smriti : An accumulation of wealth should not be made by a Shudra even if he is able to do so, for the sight of mere possession of wealth by a Shudra injures the Brahmin. (Chapter X, verse 129.)

Manu Smriti : Merely to serve the Brahmins is declared to be the most excellent occupation of a Shudra. (Chapter X, verses 121-125.)

Untouchability and Sati (widow-burning), as the Shankaracharya of Puri puts it, are part of the Hindu religion (" Honest Enemy is better than Dishonest friend "—DV editorial, May, 1, 1988). It is this desperation that has driven lakhs of Untouchables to mass conversion to Buddhism, Christianity and Islam. And this conversion is going on even to this day because the Untouchables think that this is the only way to attain self-respect. This was the reason for the instant popularity of Buddhism which was nothing but a revolt against the Hindu caste system.

The caste system is, if anything, became more powerful in " independent " India than it was in the British India having become the core of the new politics. Dr. M. N. Srinivas says: " Caste remains an institution of prodigious strength, it will take lot of beating before it will die ". Prof. Herold Isaacs has a gloomier view of the things when he says : " Almost everything that has happened in the new politics of independence has served not to weaken or eliminate caste, but to strengthen it."

Thus in " Hindu India " we have a first-class, second-class, third-class, fourth-class and even a fifth-class citizen as per the four varnas (castes) of Brahmins, Kshatriyas, Vaishyas and Shudras with the Untouchables (out-castes) called as the "Ati-Shudras," or "Panchamas".

Wheels within wheels

A foreigner may ask: "Is it so difficult to abolish castes? After all there are only four divisions". The *chaturvarna* or the four-fold division is only for outside purposes. But it is so cunningly devised that there are wheels within wheels. Each major caste is divided into hundreds of sub-castes and is further divided into hundreds of sub sub-castes and all of them engaged in an everlasting mortal battle against each other. The very function of the caste is distrust of the other caste. Distrust leads to hatred and hatred leads to violence.

In Karnataka, the Vokkaligas and Lingayats have been in a perpetual state of warfare as in Andhra Pradesh between Reddys and Khammas. And this fight between two "major communities" or "dominant castes" is always encouraged by the Brahmins as part of their great game of divide and rule so that they can continue to enjoy the status quo while the rivals are busy sniping. This is the case at all levels of this Hindu society right from a village to the national level. And the country's very politics is determined by its internecine caste war. The secret of the Brahmins ruling the country ever since "independence" is the caste system of which they are the controllers.

That is how "caste war" diverts the attention of the people from "class war". That is why every caste leader is essentially an enemy of the class struggle. Because, he knows pretty well that if the caste goes, his leadership also goes. Therefore, he makes every effort to retain his caste leadership.

Kamaraj Nadar became a leader in Tamil Nadu because he was the sole representative of the Nadars (toddy-tapper) community.

Y. B. Chavan came up because he had the full backing of the powerful land-owning Marathas. S. Nijalingappa grew up as a leader of Karnataka solely on the strength of his dominant caste of Lingayats. Charan Singh and N. T. Rama Rao (Andhra Pradesh) are the other examples.

"In any traditional society, status is to some extent ascribed by birth. But no where has it been so rigidly ascribed and no where its gradations as elaborate as in India. In addition to being rigid and elaborate, social inequalities were sanctioned by the ideology of caste. In effect, caste has come to be regarded as the prototype of any system of rigid social inequalities". (Andre Beteille : *Castes Old and New*—page 229.)

"Caste" is "Class"

Thus, it can be seen from a close examination of the Indian political history that different political leaders came up in different periods solely by their caste backing and not from out of any ideological strength. The moment the caste goes, their leadership also goes along with it. Then who is prepared to destroy such a great political asset?

In a majority of places and cases in "Hindu India" "castes" are identical with "classes". Big land-holders in the country are mostly upper castes, while the lands are invariably tilled by the Backward Castes and Untouchables. In describing the correspondence between "caste" and land-ownership in Kerala, Dr. M. N. Srinivas writes : "At the top of the hierarchy were the Namboodiri Brahmins who were the non-cultivating owners (*genmi*). The "high" Nayar castes were the non-cultivating lessees of Namboodiri landlord on 12-year-lessees (*Kanam*). The agricultural labourers both tied and free, came from the lower caste like Cheruman and Pulayan and from the Panam tribes".

There are ample historical evidences to prove that the Brahmins were also landowners along with the other traditional land-owning castes like the Vokkaligas, Marathas, Reddys, Nayars etc. Hence, the Brahmins along with these castes not only belong socially to upper castes but also economically to upper classes. So in India "caste" is "class".

In the Telengana struggle (1946-51), the fight was no doubt between landlords and peasants but the same fight turned out to be a fight between the Hindus and Muslims because most of the landlords were Razakars. And the Hindu Nazis, therefore, encouraged such a fight.

In the districts of South Kanara and the neighbouring Shimoga, a majority of landlord-tenant fights ended up as a clash between

Bunts and Billavas in the former and Vokkaligas (or Brahmins) and Idigas in the latter.

Moplah Rebellion

Even in the " Moplah rebellion " (1836-1919) of Malabar, what was sought to be made out as a Hindu-Muslim communal clash was nothing but a landlord-tenant agrarian unrest—the result of decades of oppressive exploitation of the poor Muslims. Conard Wood of the University of London who made a research into this outbreak says that all the victims of 29 outbreaks were " Hindus ". " Of the 82 Hindu victims, the caste status of 78 is determinable. Of these, 64 are members of the high castes (35 Nairs, 23 Namboodiri Brahmins and 6 non-Malayali Brahmins) and other 14 castes below Nairs in the hirearchy . . . . " (*Social Scientist*—Aug. 1974.) Conrad Wood says that " It was not accidental that these victims were mostly members of the powerful Hindu high castes. Malabar, and especially that part where outbreak occurred, was throughout this period pre-eminently a land of the big Namboodiri Jenmi and the Nair official ". If the biggest landlords owning thousands of acres were Namboodiri Brahmins, high-ranking officials of the Government and judiciary were mostly Nairs and upper caste Hindus. Moplah Rebellion was not a " communal uprising " as the upper caste writers pictured but a Muslim tenant revolt against upper caste landlords.

If this was the case in Malabar then, the same was true of the rest of " Hindu India " also. The SC/ST/BCs hated the upper castes—not only because they were hierarchically " higher " but also economically powerful and this naturally bred jealousy and hatred. Caste hatred, therefore, is class anatagonism.

The Hindu caste system, which is essentially a device to preserve the positions and privileges of the upper castes, cannot therefore be destroyed merely by the Marxian theory of class struggle. Caste system is thus the single biggest safety valve against any revolution.

Dr. M. Parvathamma, herself a Scheduled Caste and a noted sociologist, says : " I don't see any end to all this in the next 200 years unless there is a violent revolution and I have no idea such a thing is possible in this country ".

Has the Marxist leadership taken any step to combat the caste system ? No. On the other hand, they have strengthened it.

5. KARMA THEORY

The theory of *karma* (destiny?) is the second most powerful counter-revolutionary force working against class struggle. The suffering humanity, victims of centuries of exploitation are told through sugar-coated *mantras* that if they are "poor" it is because of their *karma.* The moment the masses hear this magic word (*karma* or fate) they go into a trance. Even if there is a rebellious spirit among the "poor", *karma* systematically destroys it with its mysterious and mythical hold on the minds of the toiling millions. The "*karma* theory" and coupled with that the belief in *punarjanma* (re-birth) kills the spirit of reasoning and inquiry. It removes sympathy for the "poor" from the "educated" and the wealthy. If a person is poor because of *karma,* why should the "rich" help him? So it takes away the responsibility of the Government also towards poverty-eradication programmes. It kills even the last remains of ambition to better one's life. Everything is written on the forehead of a "Hindu": if a person wins a jackpot in a horse race, it is attributed to this invisible writings on the forehead. If a busload of pilgrims die while the vehicle plunges down on its tortuous road to the "holy" Tirupati Hills, that is also due to their *karma.* If one dies in a plane crash that is also his *karma.*

Arun Shourie says: "Suffering is an illusion. Marriage is not for companionship but for procreation. It drives hypocrisy into our very being. The vulgar notions of *karma* are a handy balm for the well off—the parasites. The *karma* suits the rulers". (*Hinduism: Essence and Consequence*, Vikas, 1979, p. 144 to 163.)

The magic of *karma* has a readymade answer to every problem in "Hindu India". Dr. Gilbert Slater in his book, *Dravidian Element in Indian Culture*, says: "The doctrine of *karma* is doubtless valuable, in assisting a man to bear his own misfortunes with equanimity, but to the outsider its effect is enabling him to look complacently on the sufferings of others is even more marked. Politically, it is an anti-democratic force, as it tends to blunt indignation and nullify protests against social justice. What valid objection is there to the privileged position of the Brahmin and to the social degradation of the Pariah or the Chandala, if the Brahmin was born a Brahmin because of his previous virtue, and the Pariah either by way of promotion from a non-human existence or as a penalty for sins committed as a member of higher caste? If, moreover, the virtuous Pariah will be born again in due time as a Brahmin and the unworthy Brahmin as a Pariah ? "

Dr. Ambedkar relentlessly fought against the Untouchable's belief in *karma.* In a fire-eating fury, he said : " Your humiliations are a matter of pride with others. You are made to suffer wants, privations, and humiliations not because it was pre-ordained by sins committed in your previous birth, but because of the ever-powering tyranny and treachery of those above you .... Do not believe in fate. Believe in your strength. " (*Dr. B. R. Ambedkar : Life and Mission :* Dhannanjay Keer.)

Dr. S. Radhakrishnan, called a " philosopher-statesman " who later beame the President of India, in his book, *The Hindu view of life*, says : " Unfortunately the theory of *karma* became confused with fatality in India when man himself grew feeble and was disinclined to do his best. It was made an excuse for inertia and timidity and was termed into a message of despair and not of hope. " Even a Brahmin like Radhakrishnan had to admit the sins of *karma.*

Lazy lots

The *karma* theory has made the Indians one of the laziest lots in the world. They are not a people in hurry, like the Japanese who are impatient to achieve something in their life-time. In " Hindu India " everything is reserved for the next life, because that is what is written on the forehead. The farmers in India are so contented with the little they grow from their rainfed lands that they refuse to take to high-yielding seeds or modern irrigation methods. They are not interested in developing initiative or adventure.

The belief in *karma* and *punarjanma* has played the greatest havoc in the economic life of the country. It is said that out of the 365 days in a year, Indians " go " to office only for 65 days, that too half-heartedly. The other 300 days are spent in different types of easy-goings—holidays for Hindu festivals, Christian and Muslim festivals, national events like the Republic Day, Independence Day etc., deaths of national leaders, Sundays and " Second Saturdays ", sports and games, casual leave for 15 days, privilege leave for one month, sick leave and added to this " French leave " all make a grand total of 300 days. And if at all they " go " to the office, much of the time is spent in gossiping around tea stalls. All play and no work, because the work is reserved for the next birth in which the pending files shall be disposed off ! No other country has so many holidays in the world. That is why the Indians have become the laziest people on earth.

That is why all the enemies of " class struggle " like the big landlords, capitalists pour money on temples, build new ones, and renovate the old ones. The Birlas, the country's biggest business house, have built a Rs. 30-lakh temple at Hyderabad. The Birlas also had built the famous "Birla Mandir" in Delhi. Similarly, every capitalist is associated with one temple or the other. You go to any famous temple in India and you will find prominently displayed boards at the very entrance announcing donations from big business houses.

" Hindus " unlike the Christians and Muslims do not confine their religious fervour to their houses but carry it wherever they go—including government offices, public-sector factories and every other conceivable place.

Has the Marxist leadership done anything to destroy this dangerous *karma* ? Nothing.

6. MILLION GODS

Apart from the ingeniously devised caste system, the Hindu religion has produced many more counter-revolutionary agents who stand guard against any class war erupting in this country. Christianity and Islam, the two other major religions of the world, have only one god each. But it is only in India that the Hindus have 330 million gods—metal gods, stone gods, wooden gods, paper gods, plastic gods, monkey gods, snake gods and hundreds of other varieties of gods. (Dr. B. R. Ambedkar : *Riddles of Rama and Krishna*, DSA, 1988.) Anything and everything is a god for a Hindu : Even a chappal (a footwear). Stray cattle freely roaming about in the busy streets dislocating traffic cannot be touched because these animals are called " holy cows ". Chief Minister Devaraj Urs of Karnataka, who once made a well-intentioned speech advocating beef-eating for its high nutritive value, got into serious trouble with the Brahmins, and the " holy men " instantly denounced him for his " un-Hindu " statement. It became quite a problem for him to extricate himself from this debris of Hinduism although everybody knows that these " holy men " do nothing to look after the country's famished cattle except render lip-sympathy to hoodwink the gullible masses. India has the world's largest cattle wealth but the poorest milk yield.

Temples

Not only 330 million gods. One more was recently added to this pantheon when Sri Satya Baba announced he was not a mere " godman " (thanks to Editor Kushwant Singh of the *Illustrated Weekly* for coining this phrase) but god himself.

Hence " Hindu India " has now 330 million gods plus one, coupled with hundreds of sub-gods, minor gods, street gods—all situated within or around that ubiquitous temples that dot the length and breadth of this holy land.

Temples thus serve as the foundation seed that germinates the caste system—the very bedrock on which the edifice of this immortal

Hindu society is firmly built. There is not even a single village in this vast sub-continent without a minimum of two or three such dens of corruption and communalism, each presided over by a crafty priest, effectively propagating the gospel of *karma* to the hungry, illiterate, gullible, superstitious masses, segregated under a sanctified racism and kept poor and hence illiterate. India is not only a country where slavery is alive, enjoying religious sanction, but thanks to *karma* these slaves are enjoying their slavery.

For centuries " social reformers " have been advocating reforms of the Hindu temples as a first step towards cleansing the Hindu society. They have been demanding that these shrines of their faith should become the abodes of devout prayer and dedication. The priests officiating in them should shed the obsessional belief in their social supremacy merely on grounds of birth. They pointed out that hereditary priesthood, like hereditary kingship, leads to degeneration and cannot be ideal for promoting efficient service or real piety. But every attempt to abolish the Brahmin hereditary priesthood has so far met with frustration. A Tamil Nadu Bill to provide for appointment of Untouchables as temple priests in the State was struck down by the Supreme Court. In " Hindu India, " judges are also upholders of *Varna Dharma.*

Following this the Tamil Nadu Assembly under the leadership of Chief Minister Karunanidhi made yet another attempt on April 15, 1974 by passing a unanimous resolution urging the Centre to amend the Constitution to provide for employment of temple priests from qualified persons irrespective of caste, creed or community. Under the existing provisions of the Constitution as interpreted by the Supreme Court, these appointments had to be made from a specified denomination, sect or group in accordance with the directions of the *Agamas* (rules governing the temples) and failure to do so would amount to interference in the religious practice. This means nobody other than the Brahmins could become priests although the income of the temple is derived from the contributions of all castes as well. N. T. Rama Rao's efforts in Andhra Pradesh also met with a ship-wreck. So far there has been no attempt on the part of the Government of India to amend the Constitution to pave way to secularise the temples. Brahmins oppose caste-based reservations in all spheres except for the temple priests job.

Even a milder attempt made by the Tamil Nadu Government to introduce temple prayers in Tamil language also, besides Sanskrit, was struck down by the Supreme Court. In its judgment (June 21, 1974) the Supreme Court stayed the operation of "Tamil also *Archana*" and "Tamil only *Archana*" schemes of the Tamil Nadu Government.

The Havoc of Priests

The havoc played by the priestcraft was very well illustrated by a reporter colleague who went to cover a labour trouble at Kanpur. Striking workers had seriously damaged a factory and also tried to set it on fire and assaulted some officers. When the best efforts of the police to quell the rioting failed, the factory owner's Brahmin priest came to their rescue with an ingenious idea. He conducted a quick *puja* (prayer) to the factory god and started distributing what he called the *prasad* from the famed Kashi Vishwanath temple. Lo and behold, the violent crowd, red-hot with the "revolutionary fervour", suddenly came to its senses, calmed down and both men and women outstretched their palms to receive the "holy benediction". Nay. They even gave the priest a coin or two and quietly walked home under the spell of god. This can happen only in "Hindu India" and the incident was widely reported in the North Indian press.

Such is the havoc played by these crafty crooks who parade in the name of holy priests. To these priests, god is a business and if the god doesn't bring money, they will kick out that god also.

With their readymade remedies for all the ailments of the society, these counter-revolutionary forces cleverly maintain the status quo in the society divided into not only "high" caste and "low" caste but also "rich" and "poor"—all living in a state of everlasting peace and harmony.

If anybody thinks that people in "Hindu India" are unhappy, suffering and stricken he is thoroughly mistaken. The *karma* theory effectively palmed off by the pundits has brought them sublime bliss even in the midst of starvation and serfdom. To see the slaves enjoying their slavery, please come to India.

Any stray cases of protest here and there are immediately crushed in the name of god and *dharma*, " unity and integrity " of the " nation ". Anybody going against this established order is dubbed a lunatic, thrown away from all positions of power and laughed at by the whole society.

Our " Marxist " friends have nothing to say about these deadly forces that work against Revolution. Even a revolutionary leader like Dr. R. M. Lohia was called a buffoon by the Brahmin Press. Periyar Ramaswamy, to whom goes the credit of spearheading a powerful rationalist movement against brahminism, was not given any " national honour " although persons who colluded and worked against the freedom movement were given the highest honours by the Government of India. A stupid idiot who wormed up through the Periyar ladder and became the Chief Minister of Tamil Nadu got the highest award of the land because he was a bumlicker of the Brahmins.

Mad Dogs of Orthodoxy

How the meek and the non-violent-looking " Hindu " can be violent when anybody attacks the " sacred scriptures " is very well described by Dr. Ambedkar in his introduction to the book, *Who Were the Shudras*? (Thackers, 1970 reprint) :

" I became aware of it as never before when last year I received a shower of letters from angry Hindus, who became quite unbalanced by my speech on the subject delivered in Madras. The letters were full of filthy abuse, unmentionable and unprintable, and full of dire threats to my life . . . . It is a matter of no small surprise that when the mad dogs of orthodoxy are let loose against a person who has the courage to raise his voice against the so-called Sacred Books of the Hindus, eminent Hindus occupying lofty places, claiming themselves to be highly educated and who could be expected to have no interest and to have a free and open mind become partisans and join the outcry."

7. GODMEN

The fourth most important category of counter-revolutionary forces is that powerful tribe of *kavi*-clad " godmen " called by different names : jagadgurus, acharyas, babas, anandas, matadipatis, yogis, maharshis, siddis, his holiness, balayogis, swamis and such other charlatans who abound in this " holy country " misleading the humanity and enjoying a luxurious and lecherous life, lavishly promising everything to the gullible masses. They interpret everything in life and the whole Hindu society revolves round these " mystics."

A Hindu may live without a god but never without a godman. A " devout Hindu " will not mind if his favourite god is criticised, abused or even insulted but he will never stomach his favourite godman being criticised. Every Prime Minister of India had one or many personal godmen. Mrs. Indira Gandhi fell on the feet of many such " holy men ". " Total Revolutionary " Jayaprakash Naryan was keeping the portrait of Ananda Mai in his bedroom.

" India's whizz-kid, 15-year-old Guru Maharaj, self-styled perfect-master—residing in a 25,000-pound mansion in Highgate and rides in a Rolls Royce decked with flowers on ceremonial occasions .... Asked to explain the boy saint's lavish mode of living, one of his disciples is reported to have said he does not ask for this treatment. We do it because we love him." (Frank Moraes in *Sunday Standard*, July 22, 1973.) Such is the luxury and the lavish living of these frauds who have successfully spread their net to catch the gullible and the idiots in the capitalist world. Dhirendra Brahmachari, Chandra Swami had highest political contacts.

Guru Cult

The " Guru Cult " is becoming even more dangerous than the irrational religious fervour. Commenting on this growing tendency towards occultism among the " educated " classes of India, a noted Brahmin and a " rationalist ", R. P. Paranjpye, says : " In this land of universal gullibility any person who is sufficiently eccentric is sure to get a following. If he be enterprising enough he will even be able to spread his fame beyond the bounds of India". (*Reason*, Oct. - Nov. 1934.) Paranjpye reveals the tricks of trade of these gurus and says that "whole business is a tissue of organised conscious deceit. Few are conscious hypocrites, a few others are self-deceived, while the vast majority of people who have a vague fascination for all that is occult and against reason and satisfy this bent in the way that offers itself"

"Marxists" have done nothing to expose this godmen. On the other hand, we have reports about "Marxists" in Bengal having their own godmen.

Soothsayers

Coupled with these godmen are the fifth category of counter-revolutionaries—namely a mighty army of astrologers, soothsayers, palmists, astro-palmists, pundits, planet-gazers, bird-watchers, witchcraft, sorcerors, black-magicians and a host of such humbugs, thugs and pindaris who practically run this country from moment to moment and who are consulted even by the highest authorities in the country.

No work is done in the country without consulting the astrologer who fixes the auspicious hour for marriage, house-warming, christening ceremony of the new-born babe, launching of a new venture, opening of a shop and even the timing of death. The wonder of all wonders is that even State functions are fixed on consulting an astrologer in this "secular" country. Whether it be laying the foundation for a new hydro-electric project or the opening of a new railway line, a *kavi*-clad pundit must be present to break the coconut to herald the auspicious time.

A Scientific Adviser to the Government of India, Dr. Bhagavantam, even refused to be operated upon by his surgeon without the presence of his favourite baba beside his bed. Many Indian businessmen, including some quite distinguished ones consult astrologers rather than economists, J. R. D. Tata, India's top-most industrialist, said "....this penchant for consulting astrologers in our country lies in the fact that economists usually find it easier and safer to explain past happenings than to predict coming events which astrologers are ready to do, in addition to ensuring both propitious action and timing, some times with disastrous results ", he said. (*Deccan Herald*, Oct. 31, 1973.)

A noted Bangalore astrologer, B. V. Raman, once had the audacity to tell this writer that the Government of India had consulted him every time before deciding on marching the Army into Pakistan in the two Indo-Pak wars. Instead of putting long-distance telephone calls to consult this soothsayer in Bangalore, the Government of India could have better taken him into the Central Cabinet itself so that it could have the benefit of his consultation on every vital national decision. That India is full of such idiots in decision-making places has pushed the country to such a depth.

Nehru's Bluffs

It may be shocking to know that even a " socialist " and a self-styled atheist, Prime Minister Jawaharlal Nehru, was made to believe in this nonsense in the evening of his life. Durga Das in his book, *India from Curzon to Nehru and after*, says : " Not many weeks after the Chinese launched their aggression, Nehru was in a mood to listen to the astrologer. But the Pandit's words were hardly comforting. Nehru's life-span was over, he pronounced. Only a puja (ritual worship) would prolong it. What followed was shrouded in utmost secrecy. Fifty learned priests were engaged by his admirers to perform the prescribed rites at a temple in Kalkaji, a suburb of Delhi. At the end of the daily ceremonies, the Brahmin Pandits repaired to place an auspicious tilak mark on his forehead." Durga Das also narrates how a high official close to Nehru had revealed him something that lent weight to Sinha's (Satya Narayan Sinha, for several years Minister for Parliamentary Affairs) story of Nehru's gradual drift to queer beliefs. " It is a peculiar oriental trait, this faith in soothsayers. Nehru, the iconoclast, fell prey to it in his last years," says Durga Das.

Nehru was a Brahmin first and a socialist next. This is the case with many of our communists and " Marxists ". How can India go communist with such " communist " leaders ?

Astronomy may be a science but astrology is not. If it is a science it must be recognised by the scientists of the world. In the summer of 1988, the Government of India itself conducted a *yagna* near Delhi to induce rain but the experiment failed (*Hindu*, June 4, 1988). Instead of banning this dangerous pastime, astrology has been given all-out encouragement and nothing is done in " Hindu India " without an OK from the astrologers. Every daily paper and journal in India has " stars " column to forecast our future. Science is thus foreign to the upper caste ethos. The very fact that the country has not produced a single Nobel Laureate after Dr. C. V. Raman proves that the very " Hindu " mind is unscientific, if not anti-scientific. The only other Nobel Laureate, Har Gobind Khorana, ran away to the US and refuses to come back. This is the power of the " Hindu " killer weed that destroy even the little remaining thinking power. Even in " communist "-ruled States like West Bengal and Kerala no step was taken to inculcate scientific temper.

Such are the powers weilded by these godmen and astrologers who make and unmake governments. Several such names are familiar to newspaper readers. These are the battery of counter-revolutionary forces in positions of power always in action lulling the people to eternal peace. That is why these dark forces get all the encouragement from the rich and influential because they know the value of their power to pacify the hungry and the gullible. The ruling upper castes can rule only with the power of such dark forces.

What have the " Marxists " done to expose them ?

No temple or sadhu suffers from want of funds. Many are lolling in wealth, women and wine. " Transcendental meditation " (TM) can bring instant peace and tranquillity to anybody wanting it, that too at a moderate price. An effort is being made to bring scientists and technologists under the influence of TM for a quicker breakthrough in India.

During the *Rahu Kala*, the so-called deadly inauspicious time, every activity comes to a standstill in " Hindu India ". Even the swearing-in ceremony of a new ministry is adjusted to avoid the intervention of this *Rahu Kala*. Orthodox sections in " Hindu India " can never forgive Nehru for fixing the time of the transfer of power from the British to Indians (August 14-15, 1947) exactly at the stroke of *Rahu Kala*. They say the country has been sliding downhill ever since the Independence Day because of this inauspicious timing fixed without consulting the astrologers. With such stupid people ruling India, what future the country will have?

Humbug of Secularism

Though the Government is technically considered secular no Government function begins without a *puja*. Not even in a Marxist Government. On every Friday evening, work in Government offices come to a dead halt because the staff is engaged in *pujas*. Abu Abraham, a noted cartoonist, says: "It seems to me that what we are practising is not secularism but silence," in an article, "The humbug of secularism" (*Illustrated Weekly*—August 18, 1974). Hindus spend hours together in *bhajans* (singing prayers) and go into a trance without realising that their difficulties are not because they have not pleased the god, but because of socio-economic inequalities and exploitation.

CPM Convention

Why talk of others? At a national convention of the Communist Party of India-Marxist (CPM) at Madurai, delegates wended their way to their conference venue after offering prayers at the famed Meenakshi temple. This writer was shocked to find a CPI leader from his district of South Kanara (Karnataka) going round raising funds for a temple renovation. Another Karnataka CPI trade union leader got married at the "holy" Tirupati temple. Workers shouting fiery *Inquilab Zindabad* (Long live revolution) slogans during their routine processions, stop at wayside temples and proceed only after a reverential bow to the presiding deity.

The glaring contradiction in our "communists" is very well personified in the reply given by Achuta Menon, a CPI Chief Minister of Kerala. (*Illustrated Weekly*, November 17, 1974.) Asked: "Why I am a Hindu?", Menon reveals his mind and the basic weakness of the Left movement "I am by belief and philosophy an atheist, a materialist. However, I do not deny that in personal and family life, I still continue to practice some of the social customs and modes of behaviour associated with Hinduism as, for instance, calling my children by Hindu names, joining in Hindu festivities like Onam, Vishu and Dipavali. This is nothing unusual.

The peculiarity of Hinduism is that it embraces in its fold, and tolerates, a wide variety of beliefs and practices from animism to *vedantism.* Materialism also is not ruled out perhaps." EMS Namboodiripad, head of the CPM, presented a Parasurama (a Brahmin) idol to Mao Tse-tung when he went to Beijing. Our Marxist leaders want to be " Marxists " while remaining as " Hindus ". Is this possible ?

It is clear that " communists " in India have compromised with " Hinduism ". How can the communist parties hope to instill revolutionary zeal in the workers at this rate ? Left parties may achieve momentary victory by accomplishing a successful " Calcutta bundh " or organizing a massive Railway Strike (of May 1974) or getting a substantial DA rise for the Bombay textile labour or they can stage a massive " Human Chain " (1987). But all this amounts only to " one step forward but two step backward."

Such gimmicks are meant to mutilate Marxism. This connection between Hindu religion, feudalism, capitalism must be broken. A Marxist to be Marxist must be a first and foremost a materialist, consistently materialist. Then only it can lead to militant materialism. But India's upper caste " Marxists " are neither militant nor materialist.

8. HINDU NAZI FORCES

If the above-cited counter-revolutionary forces are playing havoc with our society, their ideas are consolidated into an action-packed programme through a Hindu Nazi force known in different names but having the same content : Rashtriya Swayamsevak Sangh, Shiv Sena, Arya Samaj, Hindu Mahasabha etc. Every upper caste man has willy-nilly his sympathy with these Nazi forces. He may be in different political parties, in science or even defence forces, still his value system is Nazi. Therefore, to divide political parties into " Left " or " Right " is meaningless. In the 1988 Allahabad Parliament election, Hindu Nazis worked with " Marxists " for the victory of V. P. Singh. In India, brand names only differ but the ideological content of every party is the same. Mohandas Karamchand Gandhi might have been killed by a Chitpavan Brahmin from Pune belonging to a Nazi party (V. T. Rajshekar : *Why Godse killed Gandhi*? Dalit Sahitya Akademy, 1987) but both stood for the same value system. Indian "Marxists" did nothing to expose the Gandhian humbug. Rather they too have became Gandhi worshippers, meaning hypocrites.

With the " hate-Muslim " (and lately hate-Sikh) campaign as its trump-card, these Nazis whip up anti-Muslim riots periodically so that the SC/ST/BCs—the victims of this great game of divide and rule —are continuously kept under the thumb of the upper castes who control these Nazi parties .

The Nazi parties are financed by the big business, the American CIA and Zionist forces so that these Nazis in turn protect and promote all the above-cited counter-revolutionary forces and thereby keep the slaves of India as slaves and at the same time see to it that the slaves enjoy their slavery. Instead of fighting the Nazis, Indian " Marxists " have joined hands with them.

Role of Defence forces

Although I have not listed our Defence, the para-military and police officers as yet another counter-revolutionary force, they are indeed so.

The " Marxist " parties must note that the officers heading the military, police, judiciary and also the civil services, particularly the IAS recruited from the upper castes, are essentially Nazis by temperament. Hence there is no chance of these officers ever having sympathy for socialism. Because " socialism " is antagonistic to brahminism. That is why the value system of every upper caste is anti-socialist.

In the 1917 revolution in Russia, even the Defence Forces joined in the march on Petrograd leading to a bloody civil war under the leadership of Lenin. It was with the full co-operation of the military and the Red Guards that the Provisional Government headed by Kerensky was arrested.

Trotsky immediately after the October Revolution said : " It must be stated that at the beginning of the Bolshevik revolution the part played by the army officers was a noteworthy one. When Lenin held special meetings for the officers of the Petrograd Garrisons where they elected the commanders who were to lead the troops against Kerensky, there were very few of the new commanding officers. They were all former officers of the Tsarist army and yet a majority of them were with us". (*Lenin :* David Shub, *Ibid.*)

Is such a thing possible in " Hindu India " where the Leftists have made no effort to fraternise the armed forces and the police ? On the other hand these forces will rather mercilessly crush any uprising by the Leftists. They are doing so even now. Thousands of dedicated " Naxalites " rotting in Bihar, West Bengal and Andhra jails is a case in point. The judiciary, which has all the sympathy for notorious smugglers, landlords, tax evaders, has refused to show even a lip sympathy for the country's finest youth languishing in prison cells.

9. SEXUAL BIAS

India is called "the largest working democracy in the world". It is also called a "free country" where everybody is said to be equally enjoying the greatest freedom of speech and movement. Press is supposed to be free. But the same people condemn China as a "totalitarian country", where there is no "freedom". If India is the "greatest democracy on earth" why our men treat women, who constitute 51% of the population, worse than slaves? Why do men imprison them in a closed cell denying them even the elementary things? In the early part of 1988, there was a debate on *sati* provoked by the widow-burning of Roop Kanwar. But the Shankaracharya of Puri fully defended *sati* saying it has the religious sanction. Why do we talk of "modern" democracy and practise the worst form of male-autocracy? Wives in "Hindu India" still consider husbands as their living god even if they beat them. But beating a woman is no sin. And for this the men have the sanction of our greatest law-giver, Manu.

In no part of the world women is less free as they are in this "greatest democracy" once headed by the "world's greatest woman prime minister", Mrs. Indira Gandhi. If it is really a free country is there any independence for your daughter or even the son to marry whom she or he wants? There are innumerable people having "foreign degrees" but barring exceptions not a single one had the courage to marry outside the caste.

What about the social ostracism of the boy who marries outside the caste? Forget about marrying outside the caste. How many parents give the freedom to their sons to move with the girl whom he is marrying?

A noted writer like Sasthi Brata, a Bengali Brahmin, had to run away from "Hindu India" being ashamed "to have been born a Hindu", In his autobiography, he says: "I do not wish to live within an authoritarian structure. I find its basic assumptions repulsive and India is an authoritarian society. Hence

I disown the country of my birth because its ethos is alien to my ways of thought." (*My God Died Young*, p. 229.)

Nowhere in the world can we find such a sharp dividing line between preaching and practising. Perhaps conscious hypocrisy is the hallmark of Hinduism. A "very orthodox" journalist colleague, a news editor in the *Indian Express*, Bangalore, who used to spend a major portion of his time both at home and also office in "spiritual pursuits", was one fine morning caught red-handed by the office watchman for stealing bundles and bundles of newspapers. And this he has been doing for years before this holy man was nabbed. Newspapers in India daily report about priests themselves stealing temple jewellery—nay, even selling the very "god" for a fast buck. And this illegal trade in idols has posed a big problem to the Government.

Sexual Hypocrisy

"Hindu India" is thus a bundle of contradictions. It is a boneless wonder. They say "god is formless". But all gods are idolised, and in the paintings of Ravivarma the female of them excel our modern "beauty queens" with stunning vital statistics. Some of our Hindu godesses may even win the "Miss Universe" contest. They say "god is above all likes and dislikes". God has no wants. But all upper caste Aryan gods in our country are daily provided with cooked food, wife or wives or even concubines. Then where is the difference between god and man? They say "god is love" and a "symbol of non-violence and peace". But look at the weapons and arms of our Aryan gods—billhook, spear, sword, dagger, bow and arrow, trident, and all such deadly armaments necessary for a murderer are found in the hands of our gods. And these gods are called in the "holy scriptures" as personifying mercy. They say that "Hindu India" is outstanding in the whole world for its sublime morality. But the scriptures give vivid descriptions of the lecherous deeds of god Krishna and Gopis and many other gods (Dr. B. R. Ambedkar : *Riddles of Rama and Krishna*, DSA, 1988).

In the land of Kama Sutra and Khajuraho there is so much of sexual hypocrisy. While our temple walls depict some of the most vulgar and obscene sex acts, which are acclaimed as our great cultural heritage, kissing is strictly forbidden by the censors on the silver screen. Can there be a greater conscious hypocrisy than this? We speak of morality and ethics and the blue films have a roaring business.

Man like a breeding bull can go on as he wants. But all restrictions are placed on the female of the species. Before marriage, she has to be under the custody of parents, after marriage a servant of the husband and if she becomes a widow she will be under the care of her children. But never free. Never trusted. So much so there is a tremendous sexual suppression among women, particularly upper caste women who find an outlet in the Indian movies that cater to their inner urges.

What did our " Marxists " do to release the woman from the male bondage? Over 50% of the country's population is crushed, cramped and confined—dumb, mute, blind and deaf. What a force it will be when it is released? What did the " Marxists " do in this direction?

10. NON-VIOLENCE AND PARLIAMENTARISM

The cult of non-violence is so powerful in " Hindu India " that even the CPM had to abandon the Marxist-Leninist path to take to " parliamentary democracy ". They say they want to usher in communism through the ballot box and not through the barrel of gun. Brahminical opium of non-violence has duped the Indian " Marxists ".

One of the greatest tragedies of this country is the dangerous cult of non-violence which has been given a new lease of life by Gandhi and Gandhism. This so-called humanist philosophy terribly afraid of the proletarian revolution, has laid the ideological and cultural foundation of fascism by concocting a curious mixture of science and spiritualism with a view to bringing about a counter-revolutionary force. From a philosophical and cultural point of view, Fascism is a peculiar fusion of spiritualism and science—which many American agents are trying to promote through Transcendental Meditation (TM), Hare Krishna Cult etc. And we have been long trying to impress upon our Left leaders that Gandhi and Gandhism are the ideological prop of the Indian Fascist culture but many a Left leader privately agress with our assessment but is not prepared to say it in public or even conduct an ideological class to expose this fake non-violence. They say that if they denounce Gandhi and Gandhism, they would be hurting the " national sentiments " and may lose their little followers. What is the use of a Left movement that is not prepared to call a spade a spade ?

When the Janata took over, Gandhism became an almost national philosophy. Godse might have killed Gandhi but the Nazis found in Gandhi and Gandhism a new light and a new hope. (V. T. Rajshekar : *Hinduism, Gandhism, Fascism,* 1985, DSA). The very killers of Gandhi have now become his greatest admirers. Nazis have fallen in love with Gandhi and Gandhism which they are using to impose a new variety of sugar-coated Fascism.

It is M. K. Gandhi who gave a new life to non-violence—a cult that has over-awed even our " Marxists ", forcing them to give up their revolutionary path and take to parliamentary democracy. Non-violence is a dangerous concept deliberately popularised by the property-holders and upper castes to keep their possessions intact from the hungry mob. Upper castes want SC/ST/BCs and minorities to be non-violent while they can use violence against them.

If violence starts the very first victims will be the property-holders and our crafty priest-craft and knowing this full well they have clung to Gandhism which provides the safety valve in which they can seek refuge.

Instead of tearing the mask covering the ugly face of Gandhism our Left leaders go out of the way to assure the bourgeois that it will usher in communism only through non-violence, through the ballot box and not through the barrel of gun. Even certain factions of Naxalite groups have given a pledge to 'abjure violence'.

The magic of Ahimsa has not spared anybody and even our hard-boiled "Marxists" are under its spell. With the all-pervading mania for 'parliamentary democracy' sweeping the country, even our Left leaders have turned reformists. While Marxism seeks to achieve reforms as a by-product of revolutionary activities, the CPI and CPM think that by introducing reforms after capturing the Government through the ballot bax, they will be able to further the cause of revolution.

Lenin (*Collected Works*—Moscow—1967—Vol. 16, pp. 307-309) has clearly warned against Marxists taking to parliamentary path. By entering into such a coalition or alliance with the bourgeois parties it is not the Marxists that will gain but the bourgeois. "Opportunism is opportunism for the very reason that it sacrifices the fundamental interests of the movement to the momentary advantages or consideration based on the most short-sighted superficial calculations", he said. That does not mean that the communists should never enter into Government prior to the capture of State power. Lenin entered the Duma (parliament) to wreck it from within but to our communists in "Hindu India" contesting elections and forming Government is not the means to an end but the end itself. This is the tragedy. (V. T. Rajshekar: *Dilemma of Class and Caste*, DSA, 1984, p. 12.)

By taking to parliamentarism, our " communists " have diffused class struggle. It will not be possible to bring socialism in " Hindu India " through the ballot box. Only some hotch-potch reforms can be brought like our make-believe land reforms which is no socialist solution. Even this innocuous land reform is forgotten in " Marxist "-ruled States today.

Upper Caste Left leadership

The Left movement in the country has deliberately refrained from fighting the above cited different counter-revolutionary forces for the simple reason that the top leadership itself is in the hands of Brahmins and other upper castes.

These Left leaders have been enjoying power and position in the name of " class struggle " while in actual practice they do nothing to further the class struggle. *The Left leadership can be therefore directly accused of betraying the country's working class.* Ask them : " Why are you not attacking this religious bigotry and the caste system ? " The reply is : " The Leftists are above these petty things. The moment a person gets convinced of Marxism, he rises above caste and religion ". This is the stock reply of our comrades.

They say this without realising that Marxism has failed to deliver the goods in " Hindu India ". This inherent weakness in the Left movement, flowing from its failure to realise the immense powers of these counter-revolutionary forces, has made it a pathetic sight. Willing to wound but afraid to hurt. Hundreds of dedicated SC/ST/BCs and minorities lured by the philosophy of Marxism have died in chill penury and cold blood devoting their entire life time to the working class and peasant movement deceived by the upper caste Left leadership.

Tokenism, not Communism

Under the onslaught of " Hindu " hysteria, the Left parties have strayed from the Marxist-Leninist path and turned into tiny reformist groups believing not in communism but in " tokenism ". They are immensely satisfied if a week-old strike leads to lockout and a final settlement resulting in a token rise of Rs. 10 in wages. They want nothing more than this. A number of them thrive on

" press conference politics " issuing lengthy statements condemning this or that move of the Government or the ruling party or giving an uncalled-for reaction to this or that statement. We don't know how such an action can be termed Marxian leading to revolution. Having taken to parliamentary system they look so tamed to voice any revolutionary slogan.

This is what Lenin had said about parliamentary struggle : " It is essential that the party of the revolutionary proletariat should participate in bourgeois parliamentarism for the purpose of educating the masses by means of elections and the struggle of parties within parliament. But to confine the class struggle to parliamentary struggle, or regard the latter as the supreme and the decisive form of struggle, to which all other forms of struggle are subordinate, means practically to desert the proletariat for the bourgeoisie ". (*Lenin* : David Shub, ibid. p. 449).

11. CULTURAL REVOLUTION

The upper caste-ruled " Hindu India " cannot have a " political " revolution of the Marxian concept unless it is preceded by a " cultural revolution " just on the lines of China. Such a cultural revolution alone can demolish the existing upper caste make-believe sham brahminic culture. *Such a cultural revolution must demolish all the above cited counter-revolutionary forces and its different facets and promote a new value system.* Such a revolution must also destroy the existing brahminical bourgeois educational system and promote " people's culture " (Dalit culture) free from all prejudices, caste canker, class feelings. Every available artist, literature, teacher, social worker, journalist, scientist and student must be pressed to undertake this most gigantic task of destroying the existing elitist culture and education and build a new one. " Marxist " parties have done nothing towards this.

" Total revolution " cannot confine to mere political and economic issues. Success is possible only if it is a cultural revolution destroying the existing phoney religion. The tribal and Dalit culture should receive full support and in fact the aim of the cultural revolution should be to make Dalit culture as India's culture.

Chinese example

Such a " religious revolution " should be made part of the " cultural revolution " which Mao took up when he realised that the fruits of China's political revolution did not reach the masses. *In China, " cultural revolution " succeeded the " political revolution " but in " Hindu India " it must precede.* A Marxian revolution was possible in China because Buddhism, an egalitarian religion, had already prepared the ground for such a revolution. Here, Hinduism is standing as a road-block. It is only such a " cultural revolution " that can pave the way for a " political revolution ". Without a cultural revolution, " Hindu India " will have no revolution. Marxian movement was a flop because our upper caste " Marxist " leadership did not realise this vital aspect. We can't say the Marxist leadership did not realise it but they have more interest in their caste rather than the country.

Indian Marxists say that scientific, technological and industrial development will automatically make religion an impotent factor in the evolution of society. Only where economic backwardness prevails, caste system and religion retard the growth. But this is not proved under Indian conditions where neither science, technology nor industrial revolution has changed the " Hindu " mind. It is not the uneducated, illiterate " Hindu " who hangs on to caste. On the other hand, he blindly follows the leadership. But it is the " educated " Indian who is argumentative, questioning, perverted. Sometimes aggressive and even violent. The two Gujarat " caste wars " were engineered by the " highly educated people." Every rationalist thought was consigned to flames not by the uneducated but by the " educated Hindu ". It is the " educated " people who entertain every dangerous thought. Give education, most upper castes turn rabid fascists. *That education brings enlightenment has proved false under Indian conditions.* It is the " educated ", particularly the 2%-strong " English-educated " lots, who are the worst skunks of the society. If the country has degenerated and degraded to such disgraceful levels, it is the English-educated people who are responsible and, not the " poor " and " illiterate " Indian.

Anti-Muslim Violence

It is because of this failure that " Hindu India " is repeatedly plunging into bloody anti-Muslim riots. A " communal riot " is a clear proof of the failure of the Indian Left movement. If SC/ST/BCs and minorities are not " Hindus " (DV editorial, July 16, 1988) how can anti-Muslim riots occur so frequently? That means the Left movement has failed to tell the SC/ST/BCs that they are not " Hindus " and that they should not play into the hands of Hindu Nazis who use them as a weapon to kill Muslims.

A " communal riot " is a revolution in the reverse direction. It is a revolution against revolution.

Perhaps, the upper castes will go on like this—neither living nor dead but just existing like animals, getting abused, humiliated and kicked from outsiders but at the same time bragging about the country's " glorious cultural heritage ". And this is how we have been existing from centuries and this is how we will be—unless a largescale war breaks out (for which there is little possibility under modern world conditions) or a foreign power imposes communism from outside. This is also doubtful. The rulers of India will neither allow the people to die which may provoke them to revolt, nor will they give them literacy which may bring awareness. Hence both ways there is no chance of an internal revolution.

THIS IS HOW MARX FAILED IN HINDU INDIA.